How to be a Mind Magician

By
Marc Lemezma

Published and distributed by
TOBAR LIMITED
The Old Aerodrome, Beccles, NR34 7SP
www.tobar.co.uk

This edition printed in 2005
© 2005 In text Mark Stork
© 2005 Illustrations Steve Crisp
© 2005 Tobar Limited

Printed in China
ISBN 978-1-903230-18-3

Table Of Contents

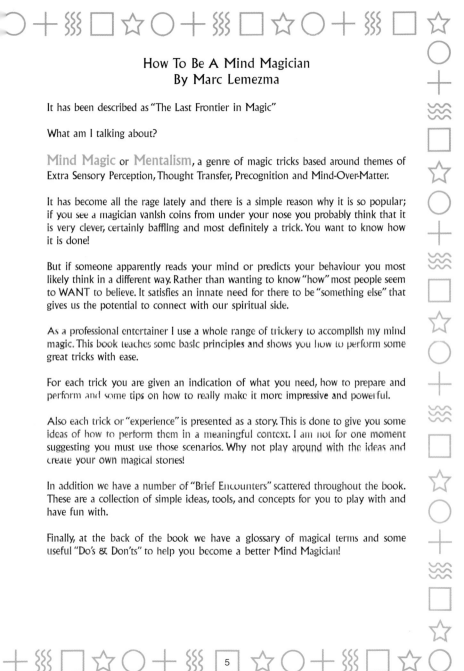

How To Be A Mind Magician
By Marc Lemezma

It has been described as "The Last Frontier in Magic"

What am I talking about?

Mind Magic or Mentalism, a genre of magic tricks based around themes of Extra Sensory Perception, Thought Transfer, Precognition and Mind-Over-Matter.

It has become all the rage lately and there is a simple reason why it is so popular; if you see a magician vanish coins from under your nose you probably think that it is very clever, certainly baffling and most definitely a trick. You want to know how it is done!

But if someone apparently reads your mind or predicts your behaviour you most likely think in a different way. Rather than wanting to know "how" most people seem to WANT to believe. It satisfies an innate need for there to be "something else" that gives us the potential to connect with our spiritual side.

As a professional entertainer I use a whole range of trickery to accomplish my mind magic. This book teaches some basic principles and shows you how to perform some great tricks with ease.

For each trick you are given an indication of what you need, how to prepare and perform and some tips on how to really make it more impressive and powerful.

Also each trick or "experience" is presented as a story. This is done to give you some ideas of how to perform them in a meaningful context. I am not for one moment suggesting you must use those scenarios. Why not play around with the ideas and create your own magical stories!

In addition we have a number of "Brief Encounters" scattered throughout the book. These are a collection of simple ideas, tools, and concepts for you to play with and have fun with.

Finally, at the back of the book we have a glossary of magical terms and some useful "Do's & Don'ts" to help you become a better Mind Magician!

A Coin-Cidence?

When people get to know you are a Mind Reader they will frequently throw the line "So what am I thinking then?" at you. This could happen at work, in the street or even in a shop when you are just buying a pint of milk. They believe their quip to be truly original (even though you know it surely isn't) but don't try and shatter their illusions; why not try and prove you do know how their mind works. This little miracle of precognition is easy and cheap to make, small enough to fit in your wallet or purse and can be quite stunning to an impromptu audience. As we magicians say "It packs flat – but plays big!"

You Will Need

Some white card, about business card size. Best get a large packet – we'll be using a few of them in the book!
A small brown pay envelope
Three different value coins and a marker pen.

The Experience

You open the fridge to find you have no milk left. You have a very dry and unappealing looking bowl of cornflakes on the table!

Kate gives you a welcoming smile as you walk through the door of the shop, you smile back. You have secretly had a thing for her ever since she started work at the shop. There is something about her eyes that just entrances you.

You grab a bottle of milk from the chilled cabinet and head off to the counter to pay. "Allwight" she says in a voice that suddenly reminds you why you decided not to actually ask her out.

"Ere , some bloke told me you do that mind reading stuff. Bet you wouldn't wanna read my mind! Ha ha ha ha ha" She emits a lewd and grating laugh. "Well I will try anything once" you proclaim. She laughs again and you cringe realising she will take everything you say the wrong way.

You open your wallet and take out a small envelope. You tip out three coins and lay them on the counter top in front of Kate. "Kate I want you to choose one of these three coins for me. Take some time and think carefully. Don't make any rash judgements." Her head moves slowly from side to side as she scans the coins, a penny, a twenty pence and a fifty pence.

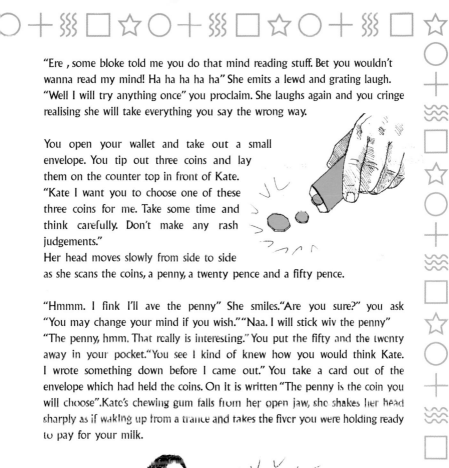

"Hmmm. I fink I'll ave the penny" She smiles."Are you sure?" you ask "You may change your mind if you wish.""Naa. I will stick wiv the penny" "The penny, hmm. That really is interesting." You put the fifty and the twenty away in your pocket."You see I kind of knew how you would think Kate. I wrote something down before I came out." You take a card out of the envelope which had held the coins. On it is written "The penny is the coin you will choose".Kate's chewing gum falls from her open jaw, she shakes her head sharply as if waking up from a trance and takes the fiver you were holding ready to pay for your milk.

Ssssh…Here's The Secret!

One of the most important things to remember as a Mind Magician is to never repeat a trick to the same audience.

This trick is a perfect example of why an audience might not be fooled more than once. It uses a principle called a "multiple out". In other words the way the trick ends will be different depending upon which coin is chosen. To prepare, you get three coins. Try and choose coins of contrasting colour and sizes. Let's assume you have the same coins as in the story.

Mark one side of the fifty pence with a large black X using the pen. Then on a business card write the following

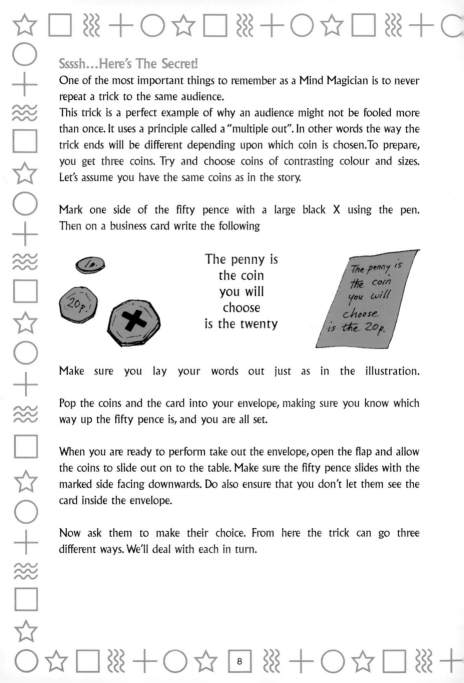

The penny is
the coin
you will
choose
is the twenty

Make sure you lay your words out just as in the illustration.

Pop the coins and the card into your envelope, making sure you know which way up the fifty pence is, and you are all set.

When you are ready to perform take out the envelope, open the flap and allow the coins to slide out on to the table. Make sure the fifty pence slides with the marked side facing downwards. Do also ensure that you don't let them see the card inside the envelope.

Now ask them to make their choice. From here the trick can go three different ways. We'll deal with each in turn.

If they choose the fifty

Remark "That is interesting. I knew how you were going to think and I marked one of these three coins"

Turn over the penny and the twenty to show they are not marked. Pick them up, slip them into the envelope and put everything away"

Ask your helper to turn over the fifty pence and see the mark you made earlier.

If they choose the penny

Remark "That is interesting I knew how you were going to think and I made a prediction earlier" Put the other two coins into your pocket and take the card out of the envelope. Keep the writing facing towards you and lay your thumb across the bottom line.

Turn the card around making sure you keep the bottom line hidden.

Your prediction is once more correct as it will read "The penny is the coin you will choose"

If they choose the twenty

Do exactly the same as if they chose the penny, except of course this time you hide the top line on the card so it reads "The coin you will choose is the twenty"

Giving It Oomph!

Now you can see why this trick cannot be repeated; your method would be blown apart.

Once they have named their selection always give them the opportunity to change their mind. Stress how this is an entirely free choice.

When their choice has finally been confirmed pause for a few seconds. This does two things. Firstly it builds some dramatic tension and secondly it gives you a chance to think about what you need to do next. You would look a bit silly turning over the twenty to show the mark that was never there!

Super Vision!

Imagine this..

You have the ability to see through solid objects. Now wouldn't that be amazing!

As a child I always wanted to buy a pair of X-Ray Specs. I had seen them advertised in an adventure comic and the thought of being able to see through doors, walls and even people's clothes was mind blowing. When I eventually managed to save up for a pair of these miracle glasses I was bitterly disappointed to find they were just a cheap gimmick.

Undeterred I present to you a way in which you can at least appear to have X-Ray vision in a neat simple trick you can do almost any time.

How?

Borrow six coins from your friends. They can be of any value, even foreign coins if you wish. The only requirement is that they have an obvious "head" and "tail" side.

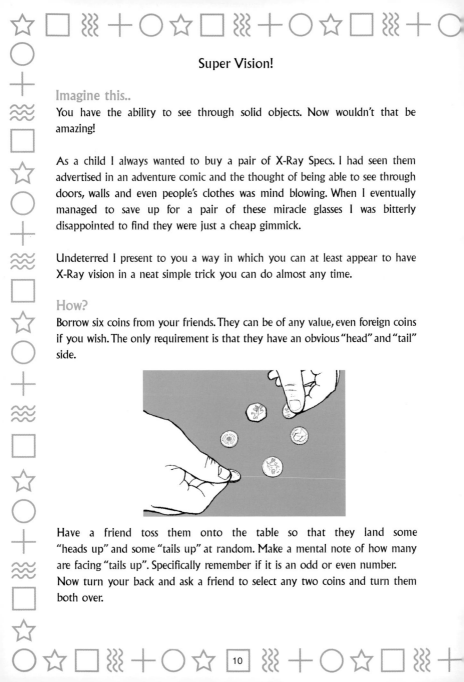

Have a friend toss them onto the table so that they land some "heads up" and some "tails up" at random. Make a mental note of how many are facing "tails up". Specifically remember if it is an odd or even number.
Now turn your back and ask a friend to select any two coins and turn them both over.

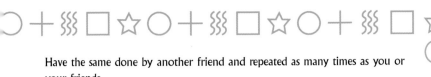

Have the same done by another friend and repeated as many times as you or your friends.

Finally have a friend choose any one of the six coins and have them place their hand over it.

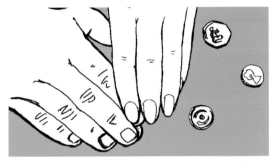

Turn around and apparently gaze at their hand as if you are trying to see through. What you are in reality doing is counting the number of "tails up" coins you can see. Again what you are really checking to see is if the number of tails is odd or even.

Now you must compare the state of the coins to their original situation.

If you had an odd number of tails before and you still have an odd number the coin under the hand will be facing "heads up". The same is true if there were an even number of tails previously and an even number now.

On the other hand if it were even before and odd now or odd before and even now the coin under the hand will be facing "tails up".

So it is a simple rule to remember

SAME = HEADS
CHANGED = TAILS

Enjoy!

Sense & Sensitivity

When your audience asks "how?" in what ways can you explain your ability to do mind magic?

To laugh and admit "it is all a trick" would spoil the atmosphere and undermine the hard work you have done practicing.

Equally to claim it is real magic would be seen as arrogant and potentially dangerous. You could end up with a cult following!

I usually admit to a wee bit of trickery, some psychology and to "being sensitive to people and the World around us". This answer still leaves some mystery and intrigue and is not entirely untruthful.

Here we present a little mystery that shows your sensitivity and intuition.

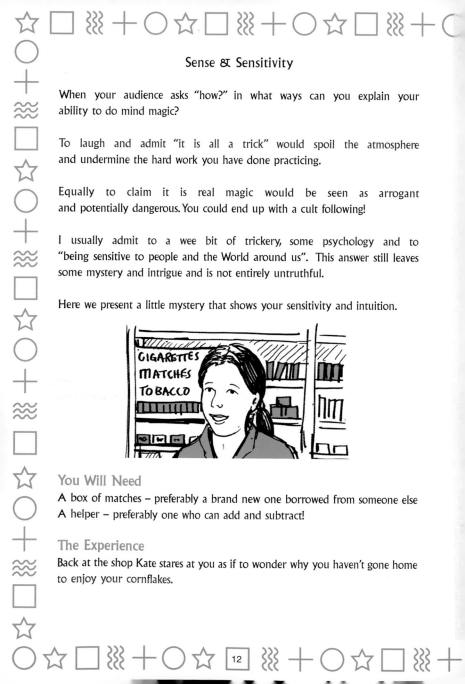

You Will Need

A box of matches – preferably a brand new one borrowed from someone else
A helper – preferably one who can add and subtract!

The Experience

Back at the shop Kate stares at you as if to wonder why you haven't gone home to enjoy your cornflakes.

"My change?" you gaze at her expectantly. "Oops sorry!" she opens the till and hands over the cash. "How did you know I was gonna choose the penny?" she asks. With a wry smile you tell her how you are "extra sensitive" and get feelings and vibrations all the time.

"I'll show you another example. You see all those boxes of matches over there choose one and bring it over please", she does so.

You point out that it says "Average Contents 45 Matches" but that is not a precise number. "I wonder how many it actually does contain." You lay the match box on your hand and shake it slightly. You pause and try again. "Hmmm, I am getting something but it is not clear. Kate as I have already connected with you I think you can help"

You ask her to remove all the matches and count them whilst you have your back turned. "Please don't count aloud and don't say how many are there just yet. Just let me know when you are done."

"Now think of the number for me Kate. You have a two digit number yes?" she confirms she does. "Good. Now add those two digits together and you have a new number. Done that? OK now please remove that number of matches from the pile and hide them from view." You then ask her to put the bulk of the matches back into the box, close it up and lay it on the counter.

"Now I could have no idea how many matches you had at the start, how many you took away and how many you have left. But you know how many are left in that box now don't you?" she nods in agreement.

You place the box on your palm and gaze into her eyes. "Ah yes I can sense it now. 36!"

If Kate had not lost her chewing gum before it would most certainly have dropped out again. As her jaw remains wide open you pick up your milk and head off home for breakfast.

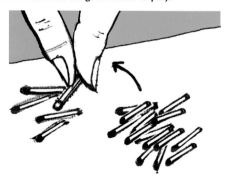

Ssssh…Here's The Secret!

A little intuition and sensitivity goes a long way to help this miracle work. In addition we do have a simple but effective magical secret at play.

Buy a box of matches and tip the contents out onto the table. Replace about ten matches, close the box and give it a shake. Get used to how it feels and sounds.

Now add ten more; you should be easily able to tell the difference between ten and twenty. Add more matches and get used to the feel of thirty and forty etc.

So now you can tell the difference between a box of ten or so matches and a box of thirty or so just by the feel and sound; but how do you know exactly how many are in there? In fact you never do. You never know how many were in the box to start with. What you do know is how many are in the box after some have been taken out and this is because of a largely unknown mathematical oddity. Try it for yourself.

Write down a two digit number say 35. Add the 3 and the 5 to make 8 and subtract the 8 from 35. Your answer is 27.

Do the same again but start with 37. The 3 and 7 total 10. Take those away and you are left with 27 again.

Try with any two digit number and you will see that the answer will always be a multiple of 9, for example 9, 18, 27, 36, 45, 54 etc.

So by combining your sensitivity to give you an estimated number of matches and the maths you can get a precise number every time!

Giving It Oomph

Once again this is a trick that must be used sparingly. If you have average contents of 45 in a shelf of matchboxes the probability is there will be 36 left after some had been removed following our mathematical process but do not assume this.

Your audience would not be amazed at all if you constantly predicted the same number and would see through you very quickly indeed.

Having said that, this effect is not limited to using matches. You could try it with a handful of coins, pieces of pasta or a packet of sweets. You could even have a random number of cards cut from a pack and use your "sensitivity" to tell how many were left.

Matchless

Imagine this..

You are out for the evening with some friends and do not have enough money for a drink. What do you do?

You can use your skills as a mind magician to win a drink by playing a game. But of course you need a sure fire way of winning!

How?

With what little money you have and by using your scavenging skills see if you can acquire four matchboxes. They should be of the same design but only one need have matches in it. These could even be dead matches. Stuff the box with the matches in up your right hand sleeve. If you have a rubber band or some sticky tape you could use those to secure it in place.

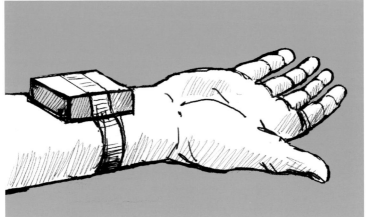

Lay the three remaining boxes out in front of you. Pick one up with your left hand and shake it. There is no sound because, of course, it is empty. Now pick one up in your right hand and shake it. Hang on, it seems to be full as you can hear the matches!

Of course this is the sound of the matchbox under your sleeve, but your friends will not be able to tell where the sound is coming from and will assume it is from the box you are holding. So it is simple. Offer your friends an even bet. They must guess which box has the matches in. Mix the boxes around with your left hand and ask a friend to chose one and shake it to see if he has found the full box. His box will of course seem empty.

Give another friend a chance, this time he has better odds as there are only two to chose from, again he fails. Triumphantly you pick up the remaining box and yes everyone can hear the matches inside.

You win every time!

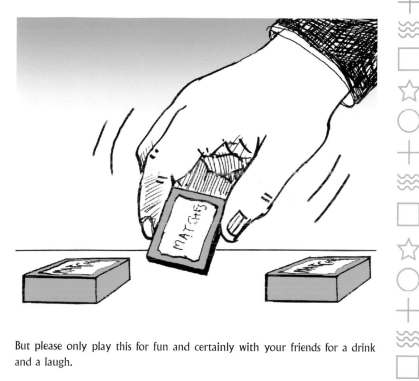

But please only play this for fun and certainly with your friends for a drink and a laugh.

A Rock and A Hard Place

Mind magic can be very satisfying at many levels. There is the great feeling you get from entertaining people and an even greater feeling when you completely bamboozle them. But nothing compares to the warm sensation you get inside when you manage to pull off something totally incredible and yet still dangle the secret right in front of your audience's nose!

This effect utilises a very bold move to create a very easy force of an item from a written list. What's more with a little thought you can adapt the idea to suit many different circumstances and many different audiences.

You could perform a version of this on stage with a bit of planning and preparation or you can deliver entirely off the cuff...

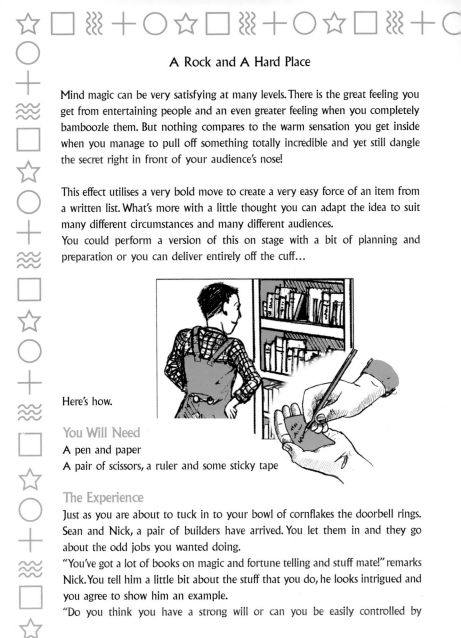

Here's how.

You Will Need

A pen and paper
A pair of scissors, a ruler and some sticky tape

The Experience

Just as you are about to tuck in to your bowl of cornflakes the doorbell rings. Sean and Nick, a pair of builders have arrived. You let them in and they go about the odd jobs you wanted doing.

"You've got a lot of books on magic and fortune telling and stuff mate!" remarks Nick. You tell him a little bit about the stuff that you do, he looks intrigued and you agree to show him an example.

"Do you think you have a strong will or can you be easily controlled by

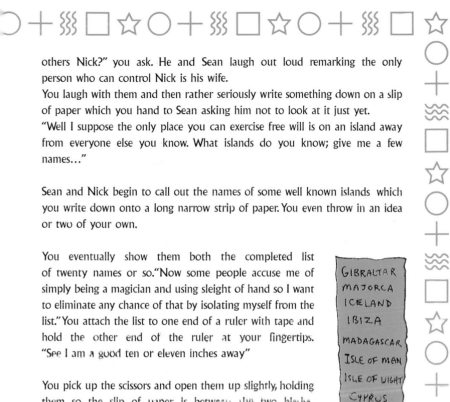

others Nick?" you ask. He and Sean laugh out loud remarking the only person who can control Nick is his wife.

You laugh with them and then rather seriously write something down on a slip of paper which you hand to Sean asking him not to look at it just yet.

"Well I suppose the only place you can exercise free will is on an island away from everyone else you know. What islands do you know; give me a few names…"

Sean and Nick begin to call out the names of some well known islands which you write down onto a long narrow strip of paper. You even throw in an idea or two of your own.

You eventually show them both the completed list of twenty names or so. "Now some people accuse me of simply being a magician and using sleight of hand so I want to eliminate any chance of that by isolating myself from the list." You attach the list to one end of a ruler with tape and hold the other end of the ruler at your fingertips. "See I am a good ten or eleven inches away"

GIBRALTAR
MAJORCA
ICELAND
IBIZA
MADAGASCAR
ISLE OF MAN
ISLE OF WIGHT
CYPRUS
SICILY
ALCATRAZ

You pick up the scissors and open them up slightly, holding them so the slip of paper is between the two blades. You slowly move the scissors up to the top of the list and then down to the bottom. "I want you to tell me when to stop Nick. I will go very slowly so there can be no cheating"

Eventually he asks you to stop. You close the scissors cutting the paper at the very point he chose. The slip of paper flutters to the floor.

"So you have chosen an island where you can go to be a free man! Pick up the paper and tell me where you made me cut please" As he bends over to pick it up you remove the remaining portion of the list from the ruler. You ask Nick to lay the two pieces together on the table to see where the cut was made. He announces that the cut was made between "Gibraltar and Alcatraz," but he looks somewhat bemused and asks what the significance of

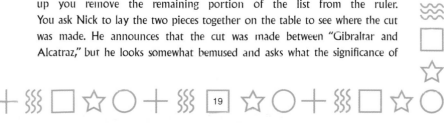

that was. You shrug your shoulders and ask Sean to read aloud the slip you gave him earlier. "Nick, I can't be sure exactly which island you will end up on – but be careful not to end up between a rock and a hard place."

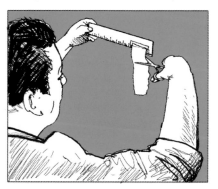

The two builders look bemusedly at each other. Then a slight smile begins to grow on Sean's face which develops into a full laugh. Nick is still at a loss but his friend helps him out "A rock and a hard place! Gibraltar and Alcatraz! Ha ha get it?" he nudges Nick who starts to realise the little joke you played on him "But how did he know I would stop between those two?"

You smile knowingly and leave them to finish their work.

Ssssh…Here's The Secret!

This one uses another devilishly simple but incredibly effective force. Start off by writing down your prediction. It doesn't have to be jokey like the one in our story. You decide what you want to force. Take a strip of paper about ten inches long and two wide. Ask for some suggestions of names of islands (or whatever you choose). However the first island you write down at the top of the paper is Gibraltar. Keep adding the names they call out and finish off by writing Alcatraz at the bottom of the list..

You can now hold the list at the top and the bottom (your fingers obscuring the two key names) and show it around to everyone.

CYPRUS
SICILY
ALCATRAZ

When you stick the slip of paper to the ruler you of course make sure the back is facing your audience so they can't see which island you are at. Now the devilish part, you hang the slip upside down, of course making sure the others do not know. Hold the scissors over the paper and ask them to tell you when to stop. In fact they can stop anywhere they like, just make sure when you cut the paper you don't cut through one of the names. It also helps to keep the cut dead straight. Now when they pick

GIBRALTAR
MAJORCA
ICELAND
IBIZA
MADAGASCAR
ISLE OF MAN
ISLE OF WIGHT

up the fallen slip the top name will of course be Gibraltar and as far as they are concerned that is where they stopped you before the paper was cut. Take the other piece off and lay them both on a table. It really does look as if they cut between those two names. Now all you need is to have the prediction read out and you are home and dry.

Giving It Oomph

You can of course use any type of item you like for your list. Choose something that fits in. It does not have to be jokey if you do not wish.

In fact you could settle for just one "dead-on" prediction by putting that item at the top of the list and screwing up the remainder of the paper.

Here is a neat Idea that really works. Place an ad in the free classified section of your local paper. Say something like "Antique pack of cards for sale. Almost complete, missing 5 of diamonds".

Now wait for the paper to come out and cut out the column with your advert, making sure your ad is the top of the list.

Then force the 5 of diamonds using the sneaky force in this book and the rest I think speaks for itself.

I told you It was cheeky!

Can You Feel The Force?

Imagine this..

You have one simple and easy to make tool, that you can carry almost anywhere that enables you to perform some amazing mind magic at any moment...

Would that be interesting?

We have already talked about how mind magicians "force" their helpers to choose a specific item whilst giving them an apparently free choice. Well this simple idea will enable you to force any playing card at any time you need.

Imagine being able to flick through a pack of cards and ask your helper to shout "stop!" They look at the card they stopped at and it matches the prediction you made earlier.

The possibilities are endless...

How?

First decide on the playing card you would like to use as your force card. I would suggest avoiding the Aces, Kings and Queens. They have a boringly predictable ring about them.

Take your chosen card and with a paper trimmer shave off just one millimetre from the top end.

Now put the card in the middle of the pack. Flick through the cards from top to bottom with your thumb. Did you notice the cards seem to stop half way through by themselves?

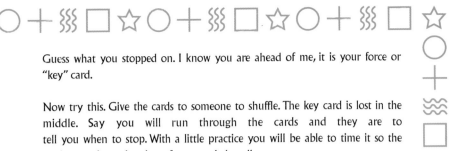

Guess what you stopped on. I know you are ahead of me, it is your force or "key" card.

Now try this. Give the cards to someone to shuffle. The key card is lost in the middle. Say you will run through the cards and they are to tell you when to stop. With a little practice you will be able to time it so the cards stop themselves just after your help calls out.

Once you master this try making up a few different force cards and keep them in your bag or wallet. Slip one in the pack when you need it Please make sure you only have one at a time though!

There are a number of full tricks in this book and my others that can make use of this sneaky force.

WARNING

Do not be tempted to have someone pick a card (using this or any other force) and then immediately name it . That somehow becomes a little too obvious and meaningless to your audience. Selling mind magic requires a little more timing, presentation and a lot of theatre!

Front To Back

As we have already found out mind magic is not simply about reading thoughts and making predictions. It is also about being tuned in and more sensitive than perhaps other people are.

Often it is simply how we choose to perform a magical effect that makes it appear to be either a prediction or a demonstration of a super sense. I recently found an unusual mathematical puzzle in an old book that intrigued me as a way to show my "abilities" off.

So here we will use this quite baffling magical anomaly to create the illusion that you have clairvoyant skills (being able to see remotely) and super sensitivity.

You Will Need
A pack of cards – which can be borrowed
A friend - who may also be borrowed

The Experience
Amongst a bustling crowd of Christmas shoppers you see a face that you recognise from many years ago. Following a brief reunion you find yourself sitting in a coffee shop with Angela, an old school friend who you haven't seen in over a decade.

You exchange stories about the intervening years and soon you both feel like you had never lost contact.

"There is something I must tell you." you begin "I have recently been dabbling with some psychic phenomena." Angela looks a little puzzled. You take a pack of cards from your pocket and ask her first to mix them and then to cut off a small pack from the top.

"Angela, you probably don't know how many cards you have there so could you please count them." She announces she has 23 cards in her pile.

"Great that is a good number for if it were 26 then what I am about to show you would be meaningless!"

You then take the 23 cards and turn them upside down and shuffle them into the rest of the pack. You hand them to Angela and have her shuffle thoroughly too. When she is done she places the cards onto the table.

"Now it doesn't take any special powers to know that there are 29 cards one way round and 23 that are the opposite way around. Please count off 23 cards again, but do not show me please" You turn your back for a moment whilst she counts out another 23 cards. You ask her to make sure the piles are nice and neat. "Now we have a pile of 23 and one of 29; that much we know. What we do not know is how many are upside down in each pile. The odds are there are more upside down in the bigger pile than in the smaller but of course we cannot be certain that is true. We can be certain of very little!"

Angela looks on as you lay your hand on each pile in turn. "Hmm, I think

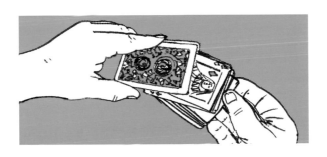

I have this pile sorted out" You say as you touch the larger pack. "I am less sure about these. I need to concentrate"

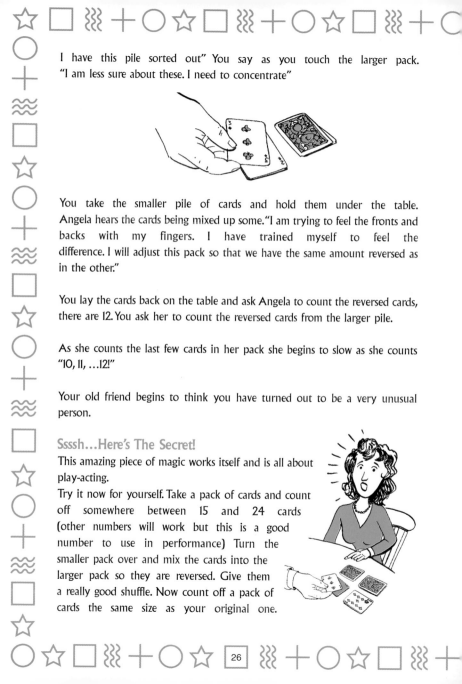

You take the smaller pile of cards and hold them under the table. Angela hears the cards being mixed up some. "I am trying to feel the fronts and backs with my fingers. I have trained myself to feel the difference. I will adjust this pack so that we have the same amount reversed as in the other."

You lay the cards back on the table and ask Angela to count the reversed cards, there are 12. You ask her to count the reversed cards from the larger pile.

As she counts the last few cards in her pack she begins to slow as she counts "10, 11, …12!"

Your old friend begins to think you have turned out to be a very unusual person.

Ssssh…Here's The Secret!

This amazing piece of magic works itself and is all about play-acting.

Try it now for yourself. Take a pack of cards and count off somewhere between 15 and 24 cards (other numbers will work but this is a good number to use in performance) Turn the smaller pack over and mix the cards into the larger pack so they are reversed. Give them a really good shuffle. Now count off a pack of cards the same size as your original one.

There is a lot I cannot tell you about those cards. I cannot tell you how many cards are in each pile. You have made a free choice.

I cannot tell you how many face up cards there are in either pile, I cannot tell you how many face down cards there are however I can tell you one thing though! There are exactly the same number of FACE DOWN cards in the smaller pile as there are FACE UP cards in the larger. See for yourself.

Sort the cards out so they are all the right way up and do it again with another number. As long as you follow the instructions and keep track of which pile is which the face down cards in the small pile will always equal the face up cards in the larger pile. This happens due to a mathematical quirk that is best left to a mathematician to explain, but you don't need to worry about how or why, just trust that it works.

By now I am sure you have figured what happens when the cards are under the table. I do not feel the backs and fronts or turn any more cards over. I just turn the whole pack around. So now my face down cards have become the face up and now we have the same number of face up cards in both piles.

Giving It Oomph

This is not a trick that one should rush. If you do It quickly it will appear to be a clever "Smart Alec" card trick. What's more you have a higher risk of it going wrong unless you pace it correctly.

So take it easy, give them clear instructions, play-up the super sensitivity part and you have an incredible miracle.

The Long & The Long Of It

Imagine this..
You have got to watch a mind magician at work...

He shows you several effects, most of which are interesting. Yet, however, he plays it completely dead pan. No variation in emotion, no humour, no light and shade.

What happens?
By the end of the third or fourth effect you have slipped into a deep sleep.

Being a mind magician is indeed a serious job. But it does not mean you have to be serious all the time and have no variety in your show.

So you need to get some appropriate light and shade and certainly some humour into your performance.

How?
Take a piece of card about the same width as, and three times as long as, a playing card. On it draw ten "heart" shapes in red just like in the picture.

If you are not an artist you can do this on your PC without too much difficulty.

Place this long card into your inside jacket pocket. Make a "key" card (as in Can You Feel The Force) out of the Ten of Hearts and place it in your pack.

When you are ready to perform announce to your audience that you made a prediction earlier that you have placed in your pocket. Force the Ten of Hearts using the "key" card (or any other force you may know) and ask your helper to look at their card, remember it and keep it in their pocket for verification later.

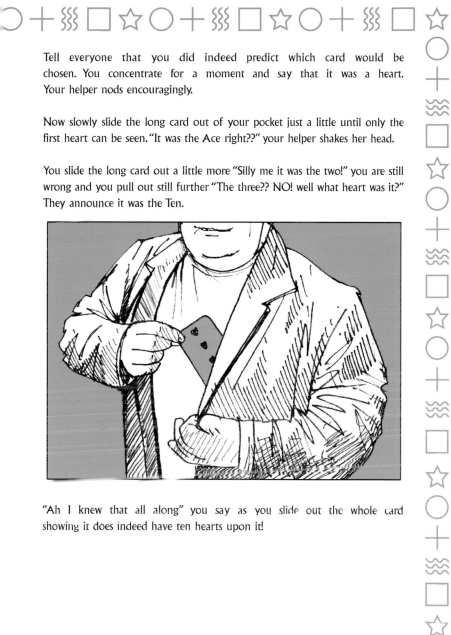

Tell everyone that you did indeed predict which card would be chosen. You concentrate for a moment and say that it was a heart. Your helper nods encouragingly.

Now slowly slide the long card out of your pocket just a little until only the first heart can be seen. "It was the Ace right??" your helper shakes her head.

You slide the long card out a little more "Silly me it was the two!" you are still wrong and you pull out still further "The three?? NO! well what heart was it?" They announce it was the Ten.

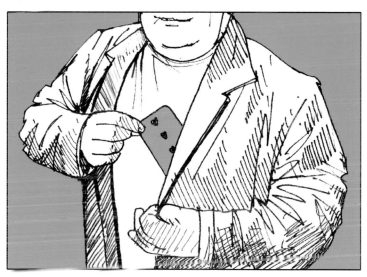

"Ah I knew that all along" you say as you slide out the whole card showing it does indeed have ten hearts upon it!

"Tuning In"

One of the biggest differences between Mind Magic and "ordinary" magic is that you don't always have to get things right 100% of the time.

A magician is defying scientific law and likes to be in control to prove he can re-write textbooks. A Mind Magician on the other hand is dealing with pseudo science, forces that are not well understood and are not easily manageable. So he has to give some proof that he is working hard to make things happen.

A performance of Mind Magic is much enhanced by not hitting target first time every time. This self-working miracle takes a rather boring card trick (much loved by drunken uncles) and makes it into an amazing feat of psychic intuition.

You Will Need
A pack of cards

The Experience
Having spent a few more minutes catching up with each other and even more putting the cards back the right way round the conversation again turns to your unusual abilities.

You offer the cards to Angela and ask her to mix them and lay out three

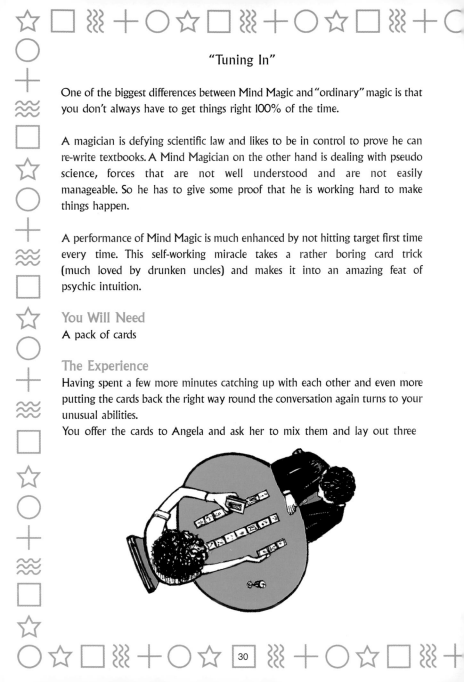

columns each of seven cards face up on the table. "I want you to think of any one of those 21 cards. Do not tell me which card and please try not to stare at

it but do concentrate intently upon it." As she does so you pass your hand over the cards with a mystical gesture. You pause over one column and look Angela in the eye "Tell me is the card you are thinking of in this row?" She shakes her head.

"Hmmm I am just trying to tune in," you say as your hand passes across the remaining columns. "Ah I have it, this column!" Again she shakes her head. Undeterred you collect up the cards and ask her to deal them out again exactly as before.

Again you try with no success, however on your next attempt Angela's warm smile tells you that you are correct at last. "Good, now I feel tuned in. Let's try one more time" Again you gather up the cards and instruct her to lay them out just as before.

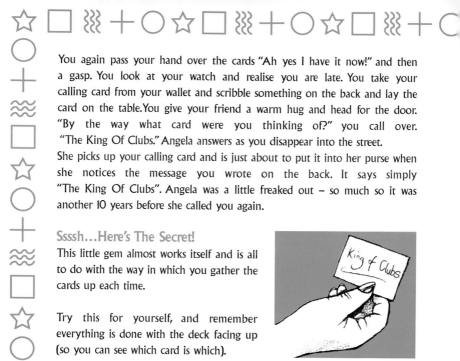

You again pass your hand over the cards "Ah yes I have it now!" and then a gasp. You look at your watch and realise you are late. You take your calling card from your wallet and scribble something on the back and lay the card on the table. You give your friend a warm hug and head for the door. "By the way what card were you thinking of?" you call over. "The King Of Clubs." Angela answers as you disappear into the street.

She picks up your calling card and is just about to put it into her purse when she notices the message you wrote on the back. It says simply "The King Of Clubs". Angela was a little freaked out – so much so it was another 10 years before she called you again.

Ssssh…Here's The Secret!

This little gem almost works itself and is all to do with the way in which you gather the cards up each time.

Try this for yourself, and remember everything is done with the deck facing up (so you can see which card is which).

Get ready to lay 21 cards out face up in three columns which we will call A B and C. Lay the first card down in position A the second in position B and the third in C. Lay the fourth card on top of the first one at position A and keep going until you have built three columns of seven cards each. Make sure you lay the cards out so that all of them can be seen.

Now pick a card for yourself and note which column it is in. Square up all three columns into piles. Put the pile with the chosen card in it on top of one of the other piles and put the remaining pile on top of the one with the card in.

So the thought of card is in a pile of cards sandwiched between two others.

Now lay the cards out again exactly as before. Note which column the chosen card is in and gather the piles up as before and place the pile with the chosen card between the two others, just as before.

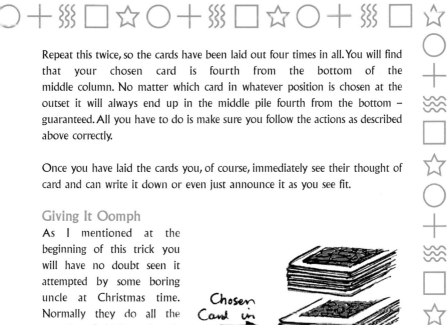

Repeat this twice, so the cards have been laid out four times in all. You will find that your chosen card is fourth from the bottom of the middle column. No matter which card in whatever position is chosen at the outset it will always end up in the middle pile fourth from the bottom – guaranteed. All you have to do is make sure you follow the actions as described above correctly.

Once you have laid the cards you, of course, immediately see their thought of card and can write it down or even just announce it as you see fit.

Giving It Oomph

As I mentioned at the beginning of this trick you will have no doubt seen it attempted by some boring uncle at Christmas time. Normally they do all the counting (which makes it tedious to watch) and announce the name of the chosen card rather blandly (which makes the ending rather lame) but here we give it a real punch.

Chosen Card in this pack.

You can play act this one all you like. Strain and struggle to try and sense which column the card is in. It doesn't matter if you "get it wrong" a couple of times because you hit the bulls-eye at the climax.

Even if you get the right column first time it doesn't matter. Just say "that's good, I wonder if I can get it right twice in a row" and if you do, amazing. Get ready to knock them dead when you hit on the card itself!

Which Way Do You Swing?

Imagine this..

You want to show your friends how it is you tune in to their thoughts so you decide to give them a practical demonstration.

Take a finger ring and a piece of fine thread or cotton about a foot long. Tie thread to the ring so as to make a kind of pendulum.

Hold the loose end of the thread between your thumb and forefinger and rest your elbow on the table. Position yourself so that the ring is dangling about 6 inches from the table-top.

Now ask a female friend to hold her hand palm upwards underneath the ring. Slowly the pendulum begins to move a little and will soon be moving in a circle around her hand.

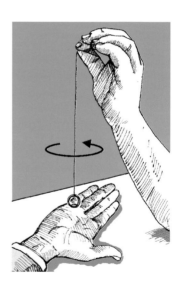

Then ask a male friend to take her place. Again the pendulum starts to move slowly but this time it clearly moves back and forth in a straight line.

You could even change places so your friends are holding the pendulum. Almost without fail it follows the same pattern, circle for female, straight for male.

Some psychics and mystics place a lot of emphasis on this mysterious pendulum. However, whilst the real reason it works is not fully understood, it is most likely some form of involuntary muscle movement that causes this strange phenomenon.

There is also some auto suggestion at work here too. Had I written the description the other way around (circle for male, straight for female) it would no doubt work that way when you try it.

Nonetheless there is potential for a lot of fun here.

You could have fun trying with any pregnant friends by telling them the pendulum will tell them whether they are to have a baby boy or girl if you swing it over their tummy!

If you know your friends really well you can spoof tease one of them by deliberately making it swing the wrong way.

"Hum I see your feminine side is very strong today! Exactly which way do you swing Andrew?"

The Number Of The Beach

We all accumulate a variety of important numbers throughout our life; be they phone numbers, house numbers, credit card numbers and even PIN codes. But the number some fortune tellers believe are most important, is the very first we get given; our birth date!

Our time and place of birth seem to be an important factor in many forms of fortune telling. Astrology and Numerology being prime examples.

By using a mathematical oddity, we can use some fake numerology to predict which resort and even which hotel destiny has mapped out for our friends.

You Will Need
A glossy holiday brochure
A pen & paper, perhaps a pocket calculator too

The Experience
There seems to be a disturbance in the kitchen. You decide to sit tight and not get involved. Instead you choose to spend a few moments looking around your friend's living room, looking at their mementoes and the books they keep.
"So sorry for the delay with the coffee. We had a bit of bother " smiles David. Anita follows behind with a plate of biscuits.

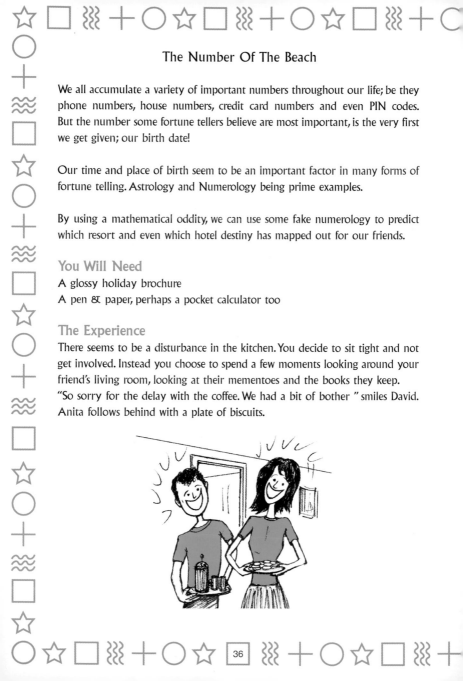

You lean over and take one, dunk into your coffee and look your friends in the eyes. "C'mon you two. You are due to get married in a few months and here you are arguing already. What's it all about?"

They explain how they have not been able to decide upon a location for their honeymoon.

"There are so many in the brochures and we just can't agree on anything"

You ask if you can help, in fact you will help them see what fate has in mind for this important holiday.

They agree, you concentrate for a moment and ask to borrow a pen and paper which Anita finds for you. "Hmm. I have a vision of a hotel. It's not clear but I will write it down"

You scribble a few words on the pad and then scrunch up the paper and toss it to one side as if it were not right.

"Perhaps some Numerology will help. Anita, think about the year when you were born and write it on the pad, but don't show me." She writes 1978.

"Now David I want you to randomly scramble the digits from Anita's year and write those down taking care not to let me see." He writes 7819 just below. "Now I want one of you to subtract the smaller of those two numbers from the larger."

David's answer is of course 5841. "Now I should tell you something about Numerology. You probably have a three or four digit number there, this is our starting number. Numerology uses just one solitary number and you arrive at this number by adding all the digits in our starting number together." You instruct them to keep adding the digits together until they are left with just one number.

"Now I want you to open that holiday brochure. Find the first hotel on the list and now count forward through the various hotels until you find the hotel corresponding with our magic number."

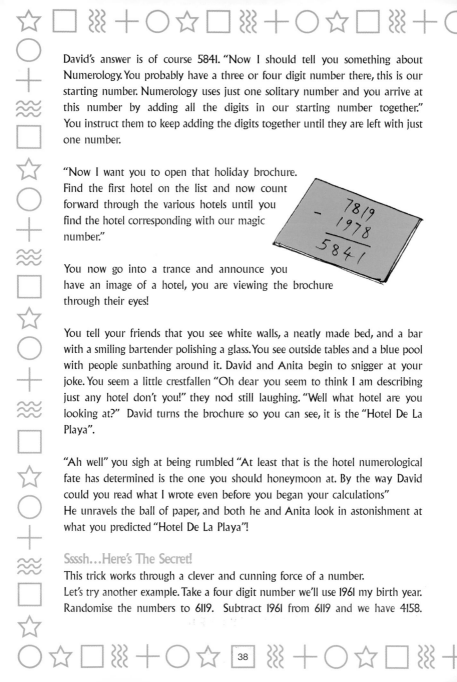

You now go into a trance and announce you have an image of a hotel, you are viewing the brochure through their eyes!

You tell your friends that you see white walls, a neatly made bed, and a bar with a smiling bartender polishing a glass. You see outside tables and a blue pool with people sunbathing around it. David and Anita begin to snigger at your joke. You seem a little crestfallen "Oh dear you seem to think I am describing just any hotel don't you!" they nod still laughing. "Well what hotel are you looking at?" David turns the brochure so you can see, it is the "Hotel De La Playa".

"Ah well" you sigh at being rumbled "At least that is the hotel numerological fate has determined is the one you should honeymoon at. By the way David could you read what I wrote even before you began your calculations"
He unravels the ball of paper, and both he and Anita look in astonishment at what you predicted "Hotel De La Playa"!

Ssssh…Here's The Secret!
This trick works through a clever and cunning force of a number.
Let's try another example. Take a four digit number we'll use 1961 my birth year. Randomise the numbers to 6119. Subtract 1961 from 6119 and we have 4158.

Add those digits together and we have 18. Add again and we arrive at 9.

In fact no matter what four digit number we start with (as long as they are not all the same!) we get the same result 9. Try a few examples and you will see for yourself.

You can of course vary this trick to suit any kind of book or catalogue, even a phone directory. You can do it on stage as part of a show or on the spur of the moment like we did in our story. All you need to do is to choose a brochure or book, secretly get a good look at the 9th item in a list or the first word on page 9 or the 9th word on the 9th line of page 9.

Then write your prediction down before any numbers are introduced.

Simple really.

Giving It Oomph

Numerology is a complex subject and one which you might enjoy researching. It is indeed the case that the numbers in your birth date are added repeatedly to arrive at one final number which determines your fate.

So using the Numerology idea, using a person's dates and talking about special things to them helps make this one of the most powerful kinds of mind magic effects around.

Of course you do not need to use dates to arrive at your numbers.

You could simply have four people call out numbers and make a number that way.

You could use times, for example as I am writing this it is just after quarter past six in the evening. So I have a four digit number 1816.

What other ways of getting a four digit number can you think of?

Date O Matic

Imagine this..

A friend marks out four dates on the pages of a calendar and you quickly cleanly and directly read their minds.

One of the great things about being a Mind Magician is that you quite often don't have to do any really sneaky work yourself. You can concentrate on performing because nature and science have some peculiar hidden mysteries waiting for us to research, uncover and use to our advantage.

Here is another mathematical oddity that can be turned into a miracle using a simple everyday calendar.

How?

The only pre-requisite for this trick is that you have a calendar to hand. It may be from any year just so long as the months are laid out in the traditional manner as in the picture above.

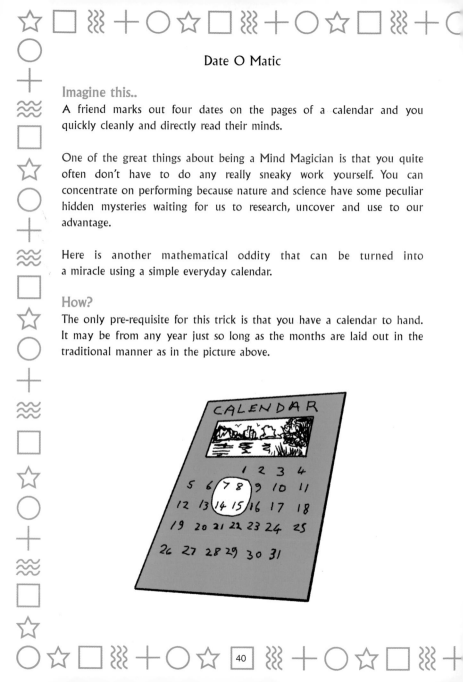

Have a friend choose a month at random and then ask them to put a circle around a group of four dates. They must, of course, make sure that you do not see what dates!

You ask them to add up the four numbers they have encircled and tell you the total. You instantly tell them all four dates.

For example, let us say they put a circle around 7, 8, 14 & 15.

The total they give you will be **44**.

Divide 44 by 4 giving 11, now subtract 4 giving 7.

This gives us the first date!

Now the remaining dates are easy to calculate – of course the next date is one day further giving us 8.

The remaining two dates are one week later so we simply add seven to our two existing dates.

So you can announce 7, 8, 14, & 15!

Of course you should do all these calculations in your head. If you use a calculator to work them out that would not be magic. But do be kind to your friends and offer them a calculator to do their adding up. This helps you too just in case they get it wrong which would mess up your maths!

From Beyond

Whether you believe in an afterlife or not and no matter if you religiously read the daily astrology columns or if you think it is all complete bunkum, there is a link (in our audience's eyes) between being a Mind Magician and those more intangible mysteries of life and death.

This gives us an enormous responsibility as we are simply entertainers. We should avoid suggesting we can tell your future or solve your problems. Yet so long as we are clear that this is all for fun (albeit serious fun) we can step over the boundaries if the end result warrants it.

Here is a most bizarre little experiment in communication with the dead. If this scares you please do read on as you can easily adapt this principle to perform some more Earthly magic if you so wish.

You Will Need

A stack of our small white cards (sneakily modified)
A pen and an elastic band.

The Experience

You have been invited to a friend's home for dinner that evening. On the way you decide to stop in the pub to pick up a bottle of wine to take as a gift for your hosts.

After getting a drink you are introduced to Sharon. She has heard a lot about you and is intrigued by your "abilities" and asks if she may see an example.
"Sharon, tell me do you believe in an afterlife?" she shakes her head.
"You know it is funny some do and some don't. In reality though most of us are at the very least curious"

You go on to explain how much there is around us that is waiting to be understood and you offer to demonstrate. You hand Sharon a pile of blank cards and ask her to sign her name across the top of one.

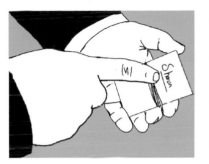

You take the cards back and stare intently at her signature. "Hmm, this tells me so much about you. You see how the O in your name is not closed but left open. That tells me there are things missing from your life, you feel somehow incomplete"

She nods. "And see how the S in your name is large and bold and yet the other letters are quite small?" you point out the details on the card "This tells me that despite your outer confidence you are perhaps less confident on the inside."

She nods again "In fact I sense a close family member who you miss greatly would that be so?" She nods and mentions her Grandfather who had passed away some years earlier.

You withdraw the card from the stack ask Sharon to lay it down on the table. You hand her the pen and ask her to write the name "Grandad" on the back and then place her hand on top of the card. "Sharon I want you to imagine

your Grandad standing in front of you now. In your mind imagine him talking to you. Can you see him??? Good!"

"Now I want you to lift your hand and look at your signature one more time."

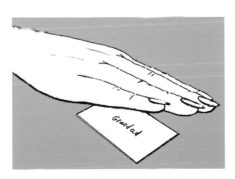

Sharon lets out a gasp and quickly drops the card. Just below her signature, where it was previously blank, is a message written in a ghostly hand. It reads…

"All is well here. Please take care of yourself"

Ssssh…Here's The Secret!

There are two main secrets to this effect, let's look at them separately.

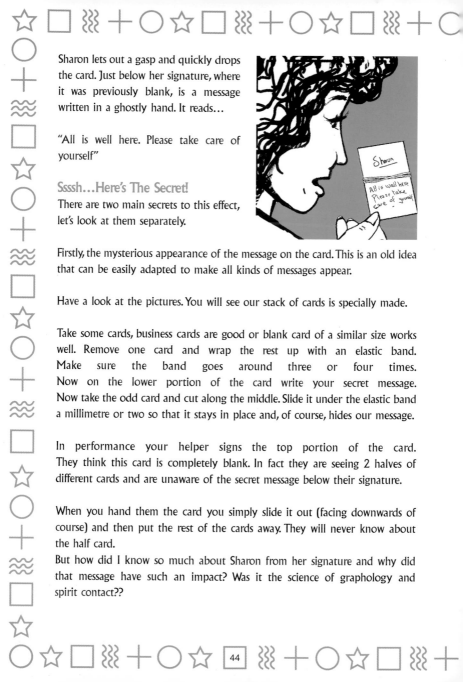

Firstly, the mysterious appearance of the message on the card. This is an old idea that can be easily adapted to make all kinds of messages appear.

Have a look at the pictures. You will see our stack of cards is specially made.

Take some cards, business cards are good or blank card of a similar size works well. Remove one card and wrap the rest up with an elastic band. Make sure the band goes around three or four times. Now on the lower portion of the card write your secret message. Now take the odd card and cut along the middle. Slide it under the elastic band a millimetre or two so that it stays in place and, of course, hides our message.

In performance your helper signs the top portion of the card. They think this card is completely blank. In fact they are seeing 2 halves of different cards and are unaware of the secret message below their signature.

When you hand them the card you simply slide it out (facing downwards of course) and then put the rest of the cards away. They will never know about the half card.

But how did I know so much about Sharon from her signature and why did that message have such an impact? Was it the science of graphology and spirit contact??

Not a bit of it. It was all made up using general statements that will seem relevant to anyone.

Ask yourself these questions.

"Do you feel incomplete and want more in life?" Most would answer yes.
"Are you as confident on the inside as you are on the outside?" Most would answer no.
Our ghostly message is simply derived from the two questions you might ask a relative from the other side. "How are you?" and "What does the future hold for me"

Again a non-specific message which will seem to fit for most people!

Giving It Oomph

I have three tips on this effect. The first is to be aware of your helper's feelings. If you know of a recent bereavement then avoid using that person. Don't try and play this to your advantage it will backfire on you.

For the secret message, try writing it with your left (or right if you are left handed) hand. This will appear shaky and not like you have written it.

Finally, whilst we toyed with the concept of graphology in our story it could be a worthwhile subject to do some research on. In fact there are many disciplines such as astrology and palmistry that once understood can help add a new dimension to your Mind Magic.

Oh and one other thing. Should your helper be that one in a hundred person to whom your graphology means nothing, do not worry! The appearance of the writing has enough impact to make your performance work.

Limb Bo

Imagine this..

Everyone expects a mind magician to be able to do more than just make predictions. Our audiences make a close association between "mind readers" and hypnotists.

Hypnotism is a very complex and intricate subject and it can be very dangerous if attempted by the untrained.

But wouldn't it be great to have a safe way to induce involuntary actions in your friends?

How?

The human body is a wonderful thing and there are some fascinating reflex reactions that a mind magician can make use of.

Try this one on yourself first.

Stand inside a doorway and with your hands flat at your sides. Now raise your arms until they press inside the door jamb. Push firmly and count from one to twenty.

Now take a step forward, do you notice what is happening with your arms?

You should feel them slowly lift up, uncontrollably. Rather freaky isn't it!

There are two great ways to work this on your friends.
You could, for example, make a bet with them that you can make them lose control by placing them in a "trance". Have them step into the doorway and push their arms against the sides just as you did.

Now have them close their eyes whilst you count down from twenty, supposedly lowering them into a relaxed state. Have them step forward and open their eyes and they will see their arms rise mysteriously.

An even better way to do this is entirely off the cuff. If you have been chatting with someone at home or in the office and they have been leaning on their arm against a wall the same thing will happen.

So stop talking , make them stand straight and gaze into your eyes as you make their arm float in the air.

But remember, this is not hypnotism at all, just a bit of fun!

Arisen!

Being a Mind Magician doesn't limit you to just seeing the future or reading thoughts. There is also the power of Mind-Over-Matter.

The two "Brief Encounters" either side of this effect explain physical anomalies that can be sold as Mind-Over-Matter or Mind-Control.

Of course there is another aspect we haven't really touched on so far, the power of Telekinesis; the ability to make objects move and even float in the air with your mind.

This is a very old parlour trick which is rarely seen nowadays. The visual effect is quite literally stunning which is made even more powerful by the fact that you yourself are not physically involved.

You Will Need
One volunteer and four other helpers
A chair

The Experience
Sharon has gone to the bar to tell her friends how amazing you are and soon there is a small group of people talking to you making those rather tedious

jokes all magicians hear on a daily basis. "Can you make my wife disappear!" or "Turn this fiver into a fifty!" or even "Can you make me lose weight?" "Ah, yes I can do that!" you say. Everyone looks puzzled. You explain that it is possible to make someone completely weightless by programming their mind and conditioning their body.

You grab a chair and ask Barry to sit. Have four people stand around him, two behind and two at the sides. "Now Barry I guess you must weigh in at about 12 stones ?" He nods "And sitting here you would be dead weight and quite hard to move. Let's try and see"

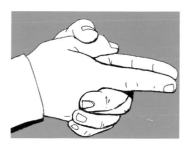

You ask the four helpers to clasp their hands together firmly and then point out both index fingers.

"Now I want you two behind Barry to put your outstretched fingers under Barry's armpits. You two at the front please bend down and put your hands under his knees."

You instruct everybody to lift on the count of 3. Barry remains glued to his chair, he is too heavy for them to lift.

"OK, now we must condition Barry's body and mind. Would the four of you please stand up.

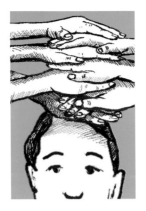

Each place one hand on top of Barry's head, one hand on top of the other, good! Now each of you please place your other hand on top and push down slightly." You look Barry firmly in the eyes.

"I want you to feel the weight slipping out of your body. You are becoming lighter, as light as air. In 10 seconds I want you all to quickly take your hands off Barry's head and put them under his arms and legs again and lift, do you all understand?" They nod...

"10 – 9 – 8 – 7 – 6 – 5 – 4 – 3 – 2 -I – GO!"

They move swiftly into position as before and lift. Barry floats up in the air a full 2 or 3 feet as if he were as light as a feather. He is lowered down to his chair and your helpers try again to lift Barry, but once again he is impossible to move.

Ssssh…Here's The Secret!

Secret? There is no secret to this at all, it seems to just happen.

If you follow the instructions and choose your helpers carefully you will get astonishing results with this incredible feat.

Of course you want to know HOW this works, there are in fact three factors that contribute to the levitation.

Firstly, anticipation of the sitter. Previously he was told he was dead weight and would not move. But just before he is made to float you tell him he will rise. This coupled with the release of pressure from his head will relax him and stop him fighting the lifting.

Secondly we have the anticipation of the lifters. Again they have been told he would be heavy and they cannot move him. Now you have told them they will succeed and they are willing to give it a go. This helps them succeed.

Finally and most importantly we have momentum. When they tried to lift before they were making a standing start. Now they are moving swiftly, their speed and impetus not only gives them more strength but also makes them push their hands in more firmly aiding them in making the volunteer rise.

Choosing the right combination of helpers is also important. Using a handful of slight young women and a 20 stone man is doomed to fail. Likewise a group of body-builders lifting a small child is hardly likely to impress.

So go with an average sized man as your sitter and a mixture of genders and shapes and sizes as your lifters. You should put the stronger helpers at the back because as the knees are lifted the sitter will tilt backwards so most of his weight will be taken under his arms.

Lastly a couple of points on your choice of chair for this trick. You need to ensure your lifters have easy access to the sitter's armpits and legs. So a low back is helpful also the chair should definitely not have any arms or sides.

Giving It Oomph

When doing a demonstration such as this one, try and play up the psychology angle. Yes physics is making this happen but the mind over matter aspect is crucial to selling this a piece of mind magic.

Finally, a word of caution. Make sure no one you ask to help has a bad back or other condition that might be affected by lifting a heavy man!

Super Strength

Imagine this..

Your friends all think you are some kind of Super-Human! And of course being a nice person you wouldn't want to let them all down would you?

A good Mind-Magician will use any means at his disposal to prove his incredible abilities, including the laws of mathematics, engineering science and good old physics.

You are about to prove you have the strength of a modern-day Samson by supporting the weight of two, three, five maybe even ten of your friends.

How?

Stand facing a wall, about an arms length away. Place your hands flat against the wall and lean into it so they take all the weight of your body. This is nothing special we can all hold our own weight.

Now ask a friend to lean against you, placing their hands on your shoulders just as you have yours on the wall. Make sure they direct their weight onto you. This seems a little more impressive, but you are about to up the ante!

Ask two or three more friends to join the chain. You are still managing to hold fast supporting the weight of four other people as well as yourself. You must have been training!

Add a few more people, as many as can fit into the length of the room. This is incredible, is there no limit to your strength?

Well of course there is a limit, however the way you stand can make it look limitless. Take a look at the drawing and make sure you have everyone stand just like that, leaning forwards with their hands firmly on the shoulders of the person in front of them.

In fact whilst it appears you are supporting all their weight most of it gets directed down the legs of the person in front of them.

The only weight you are carrying is your own and a little of the person's behind you which is all supported by your legs.

Do practice this at home with a few family members before you get the whole pub on your back

Between The Lines

One of the most common plots for a Mind Magician is to be able to "see" what is written in the pages of a book without actually looking for himself. This kind of effect is generally known as a "Book Test".

Such an effect is essentially a feat of clairvoyance or remote viewing, being able to see something remotely. This makes it somewhat different from "The Number Of The Beach" which, although they may appear similar, is actually a prediction.

Mind Magicians have devised literally dozens of methods of achieving this effect using all manner of trickery and specially prepared props. Here is a simple and effective method that requires a little preparation and lot of cunning.

You Will Need
A book...or two. Read on!

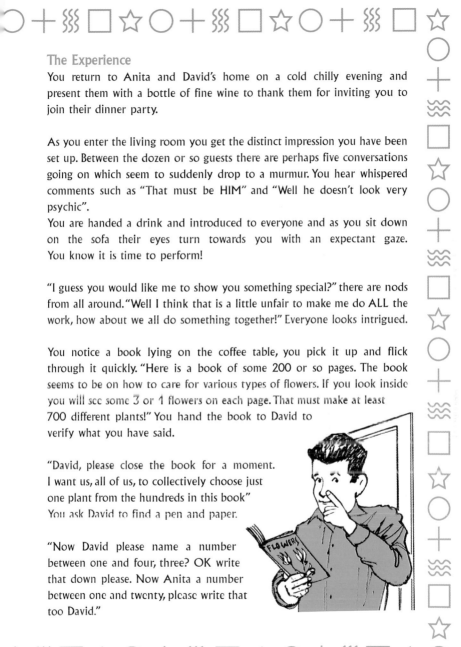

The Experience

You return to Anita and David's home on a cold chilly evening and present them with a bottle of fine wine to thank them for inviting you to join their dinner party.

As you enter the living room you get the distinct impression you have been set up. Between the dozen or so guests there are perhaps five conversations going on which seem to suddenly drop to a murmur. You hear whispered comments such as "That must be HIM" and "Well he doesn't look very psychic".

You are handed a drink and introduced to everyone and as you sit down on the sofa their eyes turn towards you with an expectant gaze. You know it is time to perform!

"I guess you would like me to show you something special?" there are nods from all around. "Well I think that is a little unfair to make me do ALL the work, how about we all do something together!" Everyone looks intrigued.

You notice a book lying on the coffee table, you pick it up and flick through it quickly. "Here is a book of some 200 or so pages. The book seems to be on how to care for various types of flowers. If you look inside you will see some 3 or 4 flowers on each page. That must make at least 700 different plants!" You hand the book to David to verify what you have said.

"David, please close the book for a moment. I want us, all of us, to collectively choose just one plant from the hundreds in this book" You ask David to find a pen and paper.

"Now David please name a number between one and four, three? OK write that down please. Now Anita a number between one and twenty, please write that too David."

You progress around the room giving everybody present a chance to name a number, David writes them all down as you go.

"We now have a random collection of numbers. There can be no accusation of collusion between me and anybody because you have each had your say. Please listen carefully. David, in a moment I will leave the room. When I am gone I want you to add everybody else's numbers together to form a larger number. When you have done that turn to that page in the book and count down the page to your own number to select one of the plants on that page. "Do you understand so far?" He nods.

"Good. Then I want you to read the description of that plant over and over, but not aloud. Just do it in your mind. When you have done that seven times please write the name of the flower on the paper and close the book. Then kindly collect me from outside the room. But please do not name any words or numbers aloud."

You leave the room and patiently wait until you are called back. You announce you saw the image of a plant whilst you were outside and you begin to describe it.

You describe the many bright red flowers, and the long pleated green leaves. You also state that this plant seems to need moist well drained soil and plenty of sun. "Does this match the description so far?" David nods but seems a little unsure, after all there were many red flowered plants in the book.

"But I did see a name. I saw LUCIFER. Does that mean anything to you?" David sprays his mouthful of wine everywhere and goes a little pale.

Anita opens the book at the chosen page and shows everyone a description of a beautiful red plant called LUCIFER.

You are handed another drink and settle down to relax for a mysterious evening.

Ssssh…Here's The Secret!

Do not be put off by the simplicity of the method for this effect. If you are a regular visitor to a friend's house it is easy. If not you may have to buy books of your own to set this up, but nonetheless it can be totally stunning.

Quite simply you have a duplicate book. Earlier in this book we were at our friend's house during the afternoon and we saw what books they had. So it was a simple matter of getting hold of a copy of your own. You can do this for yourself by seeing what books your friends have at their homes.

All you need to do is hide the book in your coat pocket, or if it is small enough, in your handbag or jacket.

As the random numbers are named add them up in your head, this is a little subterfuge as the final number is never actually calculated or announced before you leave, adding further to the mystery. Also having the numbers added when you are out of the room creates time for you to do your secret work.

When you are out of the room simply look at your own copy of the book and you are all set.

Giving It Oomph

Having said this is simple you must avoid making it seem that way. When you start to name what was written in the book do it little by little. Throw in a few facts or phrases from the chosen item or page. Then name one solid killer thing (such as the name of the plant) to create a definite climax.

Also be precise with your language. Make sure your helpers know what is expected as an error in calculation means you have no trick!

I chose a plant book for the example as they are commonplace and also usually small pocket books. This helps with the concealment.

You are not limited to books of course. Finding out which papers and magazines your friends read is easy enough so why not secretly buy a copy on the way to your next visit.

Look Left – Look Right!

Imagine this..

We all know that humans give off a lot of clues as to their thinking without knowing it. This "Body Language" or "Non Verbal Communication" can tell the trained observer a great deal about you. However, whilst not widely understood it is well known and many people try and put on an act attempting to camouflage these hidden messages when they know they are being watched.

But "The Truth Will Out" as it is not as easy as some may think to cover things up. Here is an example of how to see through the fakers!

How?

This is a simple game which you may have played before. You hand a friend a coin and ask them to place their hands behind their back. They are then to place the coin in one hand and then bring forward both hands clenched in a fist.

Your job is to guess which hand the coin is in!

If you chose at random you couldn't even expect to get it right fifty percent of the time (as in guessing which way a tossed coin would land) because your friend is an added factor in the equation.

This method, with practice, can get results of around eighty percent.

Make sure you are facing straight on to your friend. Have them hold their hands straight out in front of them, more or less at face height. Now ask them to move their hands so they are about one foot apart.

You might think their eyes would give a clue as to which hand, they would probably think the same. So if they wished to try and throw you off the scent they might deliberately look the wrong way or straight ahead.

In fact the eyes give you no real clue in most people, thankfully another part of their anatomy does – THE NOSE!

They just can't help it, their nose tends to point just very slightly over to the side holding the coin. This is a very subtle nuance and it takes a little practice to get right.

Be careful not to look at them for too long as you will get conflicting messages after a second or so. Watch the nose and go with your gut feeling.

Of course doing this just one time wouldn't be that clever, you do after all have a 50/50 chance of getting it right. So this is one trick that improves in effect the more you repeat it.

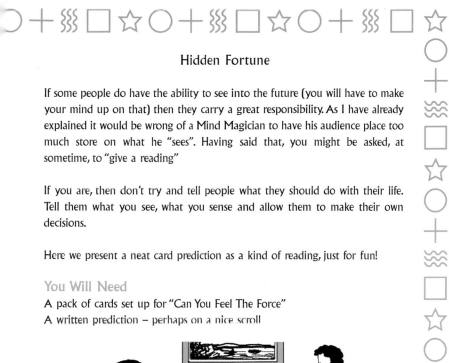

Hidden Fortune

If some people do have the ability to see into the future (you will have to make your mind up on that) then they carry a great responsibility. As I have already explained it would be wrong of a Mind Magician to have his audience place too much store on what he "sees". Having said that, you might be asked, at sometime, to "give a reading"

If you are, then don't try and tell people what they should do with their life. Tell them what you see, what you sense and allow them to make their own decisions.

Here we present a neat card prediction as a kind of reading, just for fun!

You Will Need
A pack of cards set up for "Can You Feel The Force"
A written prediction – perhaps on a nice scroll

The Experience
After your previous demonstration of clairvoyance you have just a few minutes break to enjoy your drink before you are "cornered" by Alan.

Alan is a successful man and he always seems busy. He catches you as you rest by the fireplace admiring your host's pictures and ornaments. He asks if he could have the benefit of your advice. Everybody else seems deeply engrossed in their various conversations so you agree to give Alan a brief reading.

You take out a pack of cards and a small scroll tied with a ribbon. You lay the ribbon on the mantelpiece and take the cards from their box. You rifle through the cards and ask Alan to call stop.

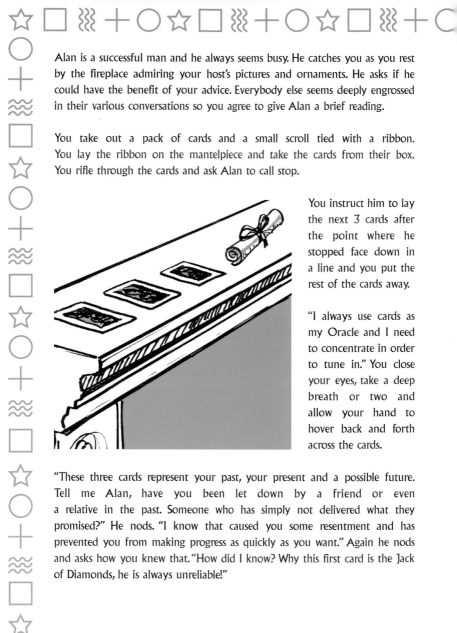

You instruct him to lay the next 3 cards after the point where he stopped face down in a line and you put the rest of the cards away.

"I always use cards as my Oracle and I need to concentrate in order to tune in." You close your eyes, take a deep breath or two and allow your hand to hover back and forth across the cards.

"These three cards represent your past, your present and a possible future. Tell me Alan, have you been let down by a friend or even a relative in the past. Someone who has simply not delivered what they promised?" He nods. "I know that caused you some resentment and has prevented you from making progress as quickly as you want." Again he nods and asks how you knew that. "How did I know? Why this first card is the Jack of Diamonds, he is always unreliable!"

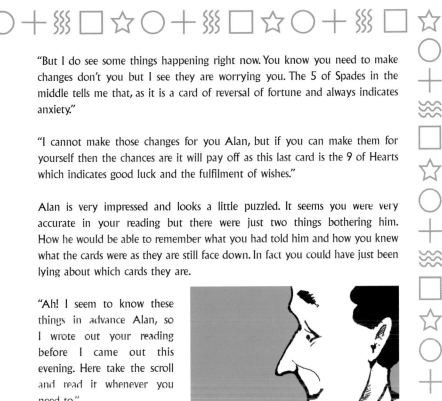

"But I do see some things happening right now. You know you need to make changes don't you but I see they are worrying you. The 5 of Spades in the middle tells me that, as it is a card of reversal of fortune and always indicates anxiety."

"I cannot make those changes for you Alan, but if you can make them for yourself then the chances are it will pay off as this last card is the 9 of Hearts which indicates good luck and the fulfilment of wishes."

Alan is very impressed and looks a little puzzled. It seems you were very accurate in your reading but there were just two things bothering him. How he would be able to remember what you had told him and how you knew what the cards were as they are still face down. In fact you could have just been lying about which cards they are.

"Ah! I seem to know these things in advance Alan, so I wrote out your reading before I came out this evening. Here take the scroll and read it whenever you need to."

You make your way over to the drinks table for a refill. Alan unravels the scroll and reads back exactly what you had already told him about his past, present and future and of course about the three cards that helped you see these things.

As an afterthought he turns over the three cards still on the mantelpiece, they are the Jack of Diamonds, The 5 of Spades and the 9 of Hearts!

Ssssh...Here's The Secret!

Again this effect has two key secrets. They are the force of 3 cards and a reading based upon facts that might seem relevant to anyone. Additional impact is gained by having both the cards and their meanings predicted in a previously written note.

The timing is also important as the force happens many minutes before the revealing of the card. When your audience recalls this trick they will forget how the cards were selected and will recall that they were chosen at random by Alan.

The force is similar to "Can You Feel" except that the short card is not one of our 3 force cards. They are the next 3 cards in the pack. When you flick up through the pack they will be left on top of the lower half where the break is. Place this part of the pack down and have your helper lay out the next three cards "from where you stopped".

The reading follows a similar principle to the one used in "From Beyond". Cartomancy is the art of fortune telling using cards and the definitions given in the story are ones which a practitioner of that skill might actually give. Think about how these meanings could mean something to anyone.

We have all been let down at some point in our past by family or friends. This is always painful.

We are all insecure to one degree or another and we could all do more to look after ourselves. We all need to change things in our life and that is our own responsibility.

The future, well who knows? You may have noticed I avoided saying what would happen. This is a good policy and it does not stop you from saying what might happen or what could happen. There is nothing wrong in giving a little hope and encouragement.

Hopefully your helper will eventually pick up on the fact the cards are not yet turned (If they don't you will have to point it out to them).

Try and make this as indirect as you can. Don't say "... you will also notice I was clever enough to keep the cards facing down" A better line might be "Oops, I seem to have left these the wrong way"

Giving It Oomph

Although you can essentially bluff your way through a reading it would seem sensible to study a little about cards and Cartomancy. This can be quite fun in its own right and a good skill to add to your repertoire.

This will allow you to make up your own scripts using your own choice of cards. You could even come up with customised readings for different occasions.

Once you have worked out your own script (use mine if you like) for your readings you could print off a few copies to keep with you and hand out to your helpers.

The Domino Effect

Imagine this..

You are put on the spot and asked to perform one of your amazing predictions. What can you do?

Well if there is a set of dominoes at hand then you can create a miracle. Here's how.

Tip the dominoes out onto the table and then ask to borrow a slip of paper and a pen. You secretly write something on the paper, fold it up and hand it to someone asking them to hold on to your prediction.

You then instruct someone to lay the dominoes in a line on the table. They may arrange them in any order they like with just one stipulation, that just as in the real game they must be laid with like numbers touching, 1 to 1, 3 to 3, 6 to 6 and so on.

Once they have laid all the dominoes out have someone announce the two numbers at each end of the line. They call out "4 and 2".

You remind them they could have laid them out in any order they wished; they agree this was their choice. You ask the person holding the paper to read aloud your prediction. They read aloud "4 and 2". Incredible!

How?

This is so simple yet so effective. Lay out a full set of 28 dominoes in a line, but pause before you lay the last piece. Look a little closer and you realise you have a choice. This last domino could go on to either end. You see dominoes actually form a continuous loop.

So, while a pen is being searched for you secretly steal away one domino and hide it in your hand. Take a sneaky peak at it, remember the two numbers on it and hide it away in your pocket. The numbers on your stolen domino will be your prediction and will match the ends when the remainder are laid out.

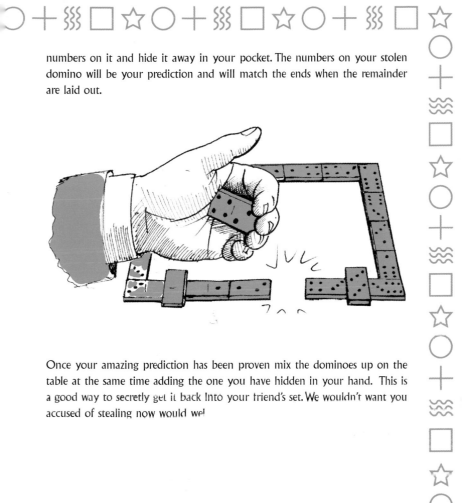

Once your amazing prediction has been proven mix the dominoes up on the table at the same time adding the one you have hidden in your hand. This is a good way to secretly get it back into your friend's set. We wouldn't want you accused of stealing now would we!

Find a Friend

Psychics and mystics talk of a phenomenon called "synchronicity". This implies an underlying but undetectable thread connecting people, places and events together.

We have already learned a little of how our birth date connects us to our fate by numerology. In fact we have many attributes which, some say, are not purely random but play an important part in governing what occurs for us as individuals.

Our given names are very special to us, in this experiment we see how they might have mystical powers.

You Will Need
8 small photographs of people
A pocket address book

The Experience
After dinner and over coffee the conversation turns to those weird oddities in life that no one can explain."

"Why does your toast always fall butter side down? "

"Where do all those odd socks disappear to?"

"Why, when I think of a friend I haven't heard from in ages, do they seem to call out of the blue?"

Several people notice you perk up when that one is mentioned. "I think I have an explanation, well a sort of explanation. Let me show you how I think this might work"

You begin to explain that you have managed to train a few of your friends who live far away to call you when you want them to. "All I have to do is concentrate on their picture for a moment or two and they seem to call. Saves me a fortune!" you laugh.

Whilst you have been talking you took from your pocket your address book. From inside that you took a bundle of photographs and laid them out on the table.

"These are a few of my friends. He lives in New York, this young lady in Belgium and the others live in other parts of this country.

"Here, look at this page I have all their names and numbers written out in case I can't raise them with my energies. Alison, will you please just think of one of those names. Have you got one?" She nods.

"I will now try and make a connection between you and one of these people. It has been said by many wise men that a person's name is, to them, the most beautiful sound they can hear."

You explain that you will randomly point at the pictures and that for every picture you touch Alison is to silently spell out one letter from the name she is thinking of. When she reaches the last letter she is to call "Stop!"

You close your eyes and concentrate for a moment. "Alison I want you to concentrate on the name, call out to that person in your mind!"

After a short while you begin to point to the pictures one at a time. Suddenly Alison calls out for you to stop.

"It seems we have been drawn to this picture by your focus open one name. Which name did you focus upon?" She announces the name Daniel. You give a wry smile. "That is somewhat intriguing..." you say as you begin to turn over all the other pictures to show they have names written on the back, each one of course is different.

"Because the name on the back of the picture you stopped me at is..."

There is a collective shudder from all your friends as you reveal the name DANIEL.

Ssssh...Here's The Secret!

This is extremely simple and easy to make up and yet can be completely devastating as a mind magic effect.

There are two secret elements to this, but if you have a good memory you might be able to dispense with one.

Firstly we need about eight photographs of normal looking people, but not people who will be known to anyone you perform this trick to. You could use some of your distant relatives or even find some pictures on the Internet.

You must also completely forget their real names, you are going to give them new ones. I use the list below

Don
Cath
Peter
Daniel
Carolyn
Margaret
Alexander
Jacqueline

Have you noticed what is special about this list? Each name has one more letter in it than the previous one. That is the first part of our secret. Write these names on the backs of your pictures making sure you get the gender correct.

If you think you can easily remember which picture you have given which name you can skip this next bit. If you can't manage to remember then you will need to mark each picture.

Try putting a small pen mark along the edge of each one. On Don's picture put it at the middle of the top edge. On Cath's the top right corner.

On Peter's on the middle of the right edge and so on around the rest of the pictures finishing at Jacqueline's which you mark on the top left corner.

Now you must write all these names in the back of a telephone book or diary and put a false telephone number by each.

Print the names so they are easily read and mix them about so that the increasing number of letters is not noticeable.

When performing simply lay out the pictures on the table (make sure you do NOT lay them in name order). Ask your helper to think of one name from your book and begin to point to the cards one at a time.

The first two pictures can be random but the third must be "Don" and the fourth "Cath" and so on. Your memory or the marks on the cards help you to know in which order to point to them.

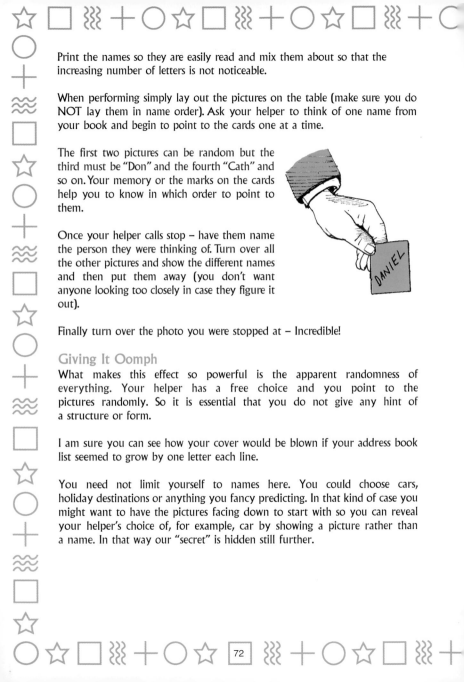

Once your helper calls stop – have them name the person they were thinking of. Turn over all the other pictures and show the different names and then put them away (you don't want anyone looking too closely in case they figure it out).

Finally turn over the photo you were stopped at – Incredible!

Giving It Oomph

What makes this effect so powerful is the apparent randomness of everything. Your helper has a free choice and you point to the pictures randomly. So it is essential that you do not give any hint of a structure or form.

I am sure you can see how your cover would be blown if your address book list seemed to grow by one letter each line.

You need not limit yourself to names here. You could choose cars, holiday destinations or anything you fancy predicting. In that kind of case you might want to have the pictures facing down to start with so you can reveal your helper's choice of, for example, car by showing a picture rather than a name. In that way our "secret" is hidden still further.

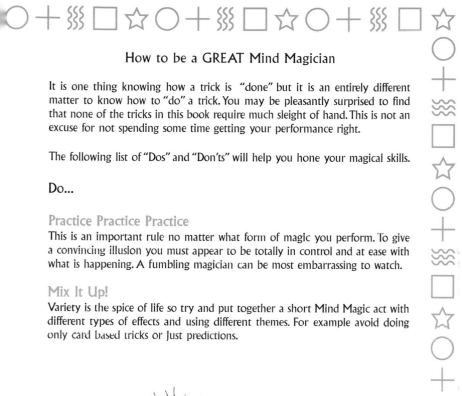

How to be a GREAT Mind Magician

It is one thing knowing how a trick is "done" but it is an entirely different matter to know how to "do" a trick. You may be pleasantly surprised to find that none of the tricks in this book require much sleight of hand. This is not an excuse for not spending some time getting your performance right.

The following list of "Dos" and "Don'ts" will help you hone your magical skills.

Do...

Practice Practice Practice

This is an important rule no matter what form of magic you perform. To give a convincing illusion you must appear to be totally in control and at ease with what is happening. A fumbling magician can be most embarrassing to watch.

Mix It Up!

Variety is the spice of life so try and put together a short Mind Magic act with different types of effects and using different themes. For example avoid doing only card based tricks or just predictions.

Involve Your Audience

A good Mind Magician knows that he must have their audience "on-side" so it is useful to involve as many people as you can. Talk to them, find out and use their names as often as you can in your patter. This book uses stories to illustrate how the effects might be performed. Put some effort into making your stories fit your audience.

Set The Mood

Whether you are performing a set show in a theatre or at the pub try and create some atmosphere. Lighting and background music are important but not always under your control. The way you look and use your voice can compensate a lot for a less than perfect situation. Make sure you speak clearly with pauses and variety of tone. Move confidently and "in time" with your words.

Leave Them Wanting

Build a good act with your best effect as a finale. Be careful not to use all your material at once. Save some for your encore or for the next time you have to perform.

Have Fun

Performing magic is my living. In time it might become your living too! Magic is about entertainment, so do avoid being too serious and "meaningful". Enjoy entertaining and the reactions of your audience but most importantly share your joy with them.

Don't...

Reveal Your Secrets

Any kind of magic is supposed to be baffling and surprising. If the secret is known then both those elements are lost and your magic is nothing. You will learn many magic secrets in this book and as your career as a Mind Magician progresses so guard them well and share them only with other Mind Magicians.

Repeat A Trick

If you do the element of surprise is gone and your audience have a greater chance of working out exactly how you did it. The result once again is your magic is NOTHING. If you do know more than one method to perform the same effect then you can consider breaking this rule as long as you can come up with a good routine that builds up the mystery.

Be A Smart Arse

So you can do a few tricks – so what! This doesn't make you a better person than anyone else. Avoid being seen as a wise guy who always gets the better of everyone else. Build a little mystique by all means but remember we are all born equal!

Be Over Dramatic

We have all seen those wailing psychics on old movies and those evil Svengali characters that control their victim's actions for their own wicked ends. They are rather too extreme to perform most Mind Magic. Build on your own character and audience rapport.

Be A Bore

I know a few magic bores. They can't wait to thrust a pack of cards under your nose as soon as they walk in the door. Choose your moment carefully. Wait for a lull in conversation or some other opportune moment or better still wait to be asked. If you can master this discipline you will soon find people enjoy your performance more and won't stop asking to see more!

GLOSSARY

Astrology
The study of the positions of celestial bodies, and their affect on our destiny.

Cartomancy
Fortune-telling using Tarot Cards or regular playing cards.

Clairvoyance
The ability to see or perceive remotely.

Effect
What you intend your audience to perceive when they watch you mimic.

Force
A set-up or action by you that causes your helper to choose the item you wish, whilst giving the impression they have had a free choice.

Gimmick
An object secretly modified in some way for the purposes of performing mind magic.

Helper
The person from your audience that you choose to assist you in your performance.

Misdirection
Controlling your audience's attention so that your secrets remain unnoticed.

Palmistry
Fortune-telling and divination using the lines on the human hand.

Patter

The script or words a magician uses during his performance to provide structure, atmosphere and misdirection.

Prediction

Your written or stated assertion about what will happen in the future.

Telekinesis

The ability of the mind to affect inanimate objects and make them move or perhaps levitate or float.